Table of Contents

Chapter 1: How does the human mind operate? 1

Explaining how the mind works: A new theory 1

The Conscious Mind 1

The Unconscious Mind 1

So why is it important to understand how your mind works? 2

How and why do humans think and act in the ways that we do? 2

Personal Response 3

Surprising Facts about How Our Brains Work 3

Improved memory 5

Better learning 6

What Happens in Your Body and Brain While You Sleep 6

Sleep is the prime time for learning and memory 7

Poor sleep makes you moody 7

Not getting sleep can make you sick 7

What is peace of mind? 11

How to achieve peace of mind 11

    1. Think positive 11

    2. Practice meditation 11

    3. Let things go 11

    4. Focus on the present 11

    5. Accept what you can't change 12

    6. Read at least twenty minutes a day 12

    7. Spend some time alone 12

    8. Relax your expectations 12

    9. Speak with a therapist 13

    10. Exercise 13

    11. Give yourself time 13

    12. Do daily acts of kindness 13

13. Get some extra sleep — 14

14. Open your feelings with someone you trust — 14

15. Take a walk — 14

16. Listen to classical or ambient music — 14

17. Practice Gratitude — 14

18. Avoid comparing yourself to others — 15

19. Look at things from a different perspective — 15

20. Love and practice self care — 15

21. Prepare for rainy days — 15

Subconscious Mind Power Explained — 16

What Is Your Conscious Mind VS Your Subconscious Mind? — 16

How Your Subconscious Mind Operates — 17

Changing Habits: Using Your Conscious Mind To Properly Program Your Subconscious Mind — 18

What are your limiting thoughts or fears? — 18

Positive Tools to Help You Tap Into Your Subconscious Mind — 19

Positive Affirmations — 19

Power of Positive Thinking — 19

Habits of Highly Successful People — 20

Train Your Subconscious Mind to Create Your Best Life — 20

Chapter 2: The Power of Words — 20

The Scary Power of Negative Words — 20

The Power of Words – You Become What You Say — 22

What's powerful about words? — 23

Chapter 3: Adversity — 25

Ways Successful People Push Through Adversity — 25

Ways to Overcome Adversity — 27

Benefits of adversities — 27

Types of adversity — 29

A Guide to Facing Life's Challenges and Adversities — 29

Chapter 4: What Is Resilience Theory? — 29

Top Factors of Resilience   30

Why Is Resilience Important?   31

What Is Physical Resilience?   32

Resilience Training   32

How to Build and Cultivate Resilience   32

Resilience and Health Conditions   33

Resilience in Children   34

Chapter 5: Main Idea- Challenging the mind   35

Maintaining the ability to challenge the mind   35

Maintaining core mentality when revisions are necessary   36

Harnessing emotional response   36

Creating the "right" mentality to have   36

Chapter 6: Fighting negative thoughts in situations   37

Ways to Stop Spiraling Negative Thoughts from Taking Control   37

One gradual habit that might help is making mental shifts   38

What situation is causing your anxiety?   38

3. What are the automatic thoughts running through your mind?   39

How can you change your negative thinking?   40

Now it's time to find an alternative to your original thought   41

Challenge yourself to make small steps instead of forcing positive
thoughts   42

Chapter 1: How does the human mind operate?

This is a common question proposed to us all. A universal answer to this question is that the human mind cannot be solely identified because each individual in this world carries his or her intellectual traits. More importantly, the power of the human mind is one thing that carries the most power to those who believe that the manifestations of the mind are one of the strongest abilities a human has. Thus, the power of the human mind allows anyone to create his or her interpretations of his or her reality, which affects the actions one takes for days unseen.

Explaining how the mind works: A new theory

The desire to understand the greatest enigma of all – our minds – has been the driving force behind many scientific endeavors, leading to the development of theories and experiments aimed at explaining the mechanics of being human. Human thoughts, feelings, and behaviors are rooted in the brain, where a complex network of cells receives information from the internal and external environment, transforming this information into our experience of ourselves, the world around us, and our relationships with it. It goes without saying that how this happens is still being explored.

The Conscious Mind

Scientists believe that your *conscious mind* makes up less than 10% of the mind's total operational power. Your conscious mind is responsible for:

- Gathering data
- Assessing and processing the data you're collecting
- Finding patterns and making comparisons
- Making decisions and giving orders
- Enabling you to respond thoughtfully to situations (rather than reacting in a knee-jerk way)
- Controlling your short-term memory

When something is in your conscious mind, it's deliberate and you're 'aware' of it.

The Unconscious Mind

The other 90% of your software is your unconscious mind. It feels inaccessible, because you're not consciously aware of what goes on in there, but trust me:
Your unconscious mind is immensely powerful.

- It runs most of the workings of your body – e.g. breathing, digestion, sleeping, heart rate, and temperature control – all without you having to lift a finger (and it controls that too).
- It protects you by trying to maintain the status quo, which is why you sometimes feel uncomfortable when you're trying to make a change. Your mind wants to steer you back to what is familiar and therefore 'safe'.
- It's the seat of your emotions.
- It's where your imagination and creativity stem from.

- It's also where your habits are created and maintained – I'll come back to that in a minute.
- Your subconscious mind obeys instructions from your conscious mind.
- It causes you to react automatically when something threatens you – you might run or freeze or as your fight or flight response kicks in.
- It stores and retrieves longer-term memories.

As I mentioned when looking at self-talk, your unconscious mind isn't rational. It doesn't make judgments and can't distinguish between right or wrong, good or bad. It simply accepts what it is told or shown as the truth, regardless of the veracity of the information. You then automatically think and feel and behave in a way that is consistent with that truth.

So why is it important to understand how your mind works?

Because, ultimately, that knowledge gives you much more control over how to use the combined power of your conscious and unconscious minds to think in a more healthy, flexible, resilient, and goal-supporting way.

The benefits include improved self-worth, far less emotional upheaval, and a much greater ability to achieve what you want in life.

One of the functions of the unconscious mind is to create and maintain habits – and that's something I'm going to come back to in my next post when I talk about how your mind forms habits – both good and bad – and how you can use this knowledge to your advantage.

How and why do humans think and act in the ways that we do?

The way the brain works
 The strongest evidence in support of the proposed brain architecture comes from predictive coding approaches in neuroscience, alongside studies based on graph theory in network neuroscience. This provides a functional explanation of the brain's hierarchical structure. More specifically, the predictive coding paradigm proposes that a brain is an inference machine, which tries to improve its predictions about the world by reducing discrepancies between what it expects and what it experiences. According to this perspective, the brain embodies a hierarchy of hypotheses about the world based on evolutionary imperatives and experiential, learned observations, which are thought to be encoded by specialized, deep pyramidal cells. The brain also contains information about prediction errors, encoded by superficial pyramidal cells, which are used to revise expectations in a bottom-up fashion. The relative influence of descending predictions versus ascending error signals is fine-tuned by their 'precision', which arises from cognitive processes such as intentional selection and sensory attenuation that ensure that individuals aren't perpetually registering and responding to all of the stimuli they receive.

The origins of the brain

The evolutionary systems theory upon which the HMM rests proposes that the brain is a complex adaptive system that has emerged from the influence of selection acting on the dynamics of human phenotypes over different timescales. Primitive, highly specialized regions that occupy the lowest layers of the cortical hierarchy have emerged from the influence of natural selection over evolutionary time; epigenetic influences and cultural evolution shape neural dynamics over generations; individual differences in neural form and function arise throughout development, and different patterns of cognition and behavior emerge from neural mechanisms that respond flexibly to different contexts. On the one hand, this means that the brain comprises ancient, relatively 'domain-specific' regions that reflect adaptations canalized by natural selection; on the other, it comprises relatively recent, highly integrated or 'domain-general' networks that are highly plastic, sensitive to developmental change, and allow us to learn about, and respond flexibly to, our ever-changing environments. In this way, evolution and development operate together to refine our neurocognitive predictions about the world, and by extension, improve our ability to reduce our uncertainty or surprise.

Looking forward
 While the HMM is a step toward integrating existing knowledge into a comprehensive theory explaining the most complex system known to man, its development has only begun. The scientific value of this theory ultimately depends on the hypotheses and evidence it generates. Central to the HMM is the need to develop testable hypotheses that bring together insights spanning the manifold sub-disciplines of psychology with theories and methods gleaned from neuroscience. Bridging these transdisciplinary divisions has long been a challenge.

Personal Response

What do you consider the biggest challenge in integrating research from these many different and highly-specialized domains?
The most difficult challenge lies in our attempt to provide a unifying and highly theoretical model of the brain that motivates other researchers to take it up for their purposes. Otherwise, there are two main obstacles at play. The first of these is theoretical and stems from the need to develop evidence-based hypotheses that span the breadth of psychology, along with relevant neuroscience research. To test such hypotheses, the second challenge is methodological – it requires computational and imaging methods in neuroscience to be wedded more closely with an experimental, questionnaire, and observational methods in psychology.

Surprising Facts about How Our Brains Work

One of the things that surprise me time and time again is how we think our brains work and how they do.
On many occasions I find myself convinced that there is a certain way to do things, only to find out that actually, that's the completely wrong way to think about it. For example, I always found it fairly understandable that we can multitask. Well, according to the latest research studies, our brains can't handle 2 tasks at the same time.
Recently I came across more of these fascinating experiments and ideas that helped a ton to adjust my workflow towards how our brains work (instead of what I thought!)

1. Your brain does creative work better when you're tired
When I explored the science of our body clocks and how they affect our daily routines, I was interested to find that a lot of the way I'd planned my days wasn't the best way to go about it. The way we work, in particular, actually has a lot to do with the cycles of our body clocks.
Here's how it breaks down:
If you're a morning lark, say, you'll want to favor those morning hours when you're feeling more fresh to get your most demanding, analytic work done. Using your brain to solve problems, answer questions and make decisions is best done when you're at your peak
For night owls, this is a much later period in the day.
On the other hand, if you're trying to do creative work, you'll have more luck when you're tired and your brain isn't functioning as efficiently. This sounds crazy, but it makes sense when you look at the reasoning behind it. It's one of the reasons why great ideas often happen in the shower after a long day of work.
If you're tired, your brain is not as good at filtering out distractions and focusing on a particular task. It's also a lot less efficient at remembering connections between ideas or concepts. These are both good things when it comes to creative work since this kind of work requires us to make new connections, be open to new ideas, and think in new ways. So a tired, fuzzy brain is much more useful to us when working on creative projects.
Insight problems involve thinking outside the box. This is where susceptibility to "distraction" can be of benefit. At off-peak times we are less focused and may consider a broader range of information. This wider scope gives us access to more alternatives and diverse interpretations, thus fostering innovation and insight.

2. Stress can change the size of your brain (and make it smaller)

I bet you didn't know stress is the most common cause of changes in brain function. I was surprised to find this out when I looked into how stress affects our brains.
I also found some research that showed signs of brain size decreasing due to stress.
One study used baby monkeys to test the effects of stress on development and long-term mental health. Half the monkeys were cared for by their peers for 6 months while the other half remained with their mothers. Afterward, the monkeys were returned to typical social groups for several months before the researchers scanned their brains.
For the monkeys who had been removed from their mothers and cared for by their peers, areas of their brains related to stress were still enlarged, even after being in normal social conditions for several months.
Although more studies are needed to explore this fully, it's pretty scary to think that prolonged stress could affect our brains long-term.
Another study found that in rats who were exposed to chronic stress, the hippocampus in their brains shrank. The hippocampus is integral to forming memories. It has been debated before whether Post Traumatic Stress Disorder (PTSD) can shrink the hippocampus, or whether people with naturally smaller hippocampuses are just more prone to PTSD. This study could point to stress being a factor in actually changing the brain.

3. It is literally impossible for our brains to multi-task

Multi-tasking is something we've long been encouraged to practice, but it turns out multitasking is actually impossible. When we think we're multitasking, we're actually *context-switching*. That is, we're quickly switching back and forth between different tasks, rather than doing them *at the same time*.
The book Brain Rules explains how detrimental "multi-tasking" can be:
Research shows your error rate goes up 50 percent and it takes you twice as long to do things.
The problem with multitasking is that we're splitting our brain's resources. We're giving less attention to each task, and probably performing worse on all of them:
When the brain tries to do two things at once, it divides and conquers, dedicating one-half of our gray matter to each task.
Here is what this looks like in reality. Whilst we try to do both Action A and Action B at the same time, our brain is never handling both simultaneously. Instead, it has to painfully switch back and forth and use important brainpower just for the switching:
When our brains handle a single task, the prefrontal cortex plays a big part. Here's how it helps us achieve a goal or complete a task:
The anterior part of this brain region forms the goal or intention—for example, "I want that cookie"—and the posterior prefrontal cortex talks to the rest of the brain so that your hand reaches toward the cookie jar and your mind knows whether you have the cookie.
A study in Paris found that when a second task was required, the brains of the study volunteers split up, with each hemisphere working alone on a task. The brain was overloaded by the second task and couldn't perform at its full capacity, because it needed to split its resources.
When a third task was added, the volunteers' results plummeted:
The triple-task jugglers consistently forgot one of their tasks. They also made three times as many errors as they did while dual-tasking.

4. Naps improve your brain's day to day performance

We're pretty clear on how important sleep is for our brains, but what about naps? It turns out, these short bursts of sleep are useful.
Here are a couple of ways napping can benefit the brain:

Improved memory

In one study, participants memorized illustrated cards to test their memory strength. After memorizing a set of cards, they had a 40-minute break wherein one group napped, and the other stayed awake. After the break, both groups were tested on their memory of the cards, and the group who had napped performed better:
Much to the surprise of the researchers, the sleep group performed significantly better, retaining on average 85 percent of the patterns, compared to 60 percent for those who had remained awake.
Napping helps our brain to solidify memories:
Research indicates that when a memory is first recorded in the brain—in the hippocampus, to be specific—it's still "fragile" and easily forgotten, especially if the brain is asked to memorize more things. Napping, it seems, pushes memories to the

neocortex, the brains "more permanent storage," preventing them from being "overwritten."
Let's look at that in a graph – the people who took a nap, were able to wildly outperform those who didn't. It's like they had a fresh start:

Better learning
Taking a nap also helps to clear information out of your brain's temporary storage areas, getting it ready for new information to be absorbed. A study from the University of California asked participants to complete a challenging task around midday, which required them to take in a lot of new information. At around 2 p.m., half of the volunteers took a nap while the rest stayed awake.
The really interesting part of this study is not only that at 6 p.m. that night the napping group performed better than those who didn't take a nap. The napping group performed better than they had earlier in the morning.

What Happens in Your Body and Brain While You Sleep

You might think of sleep as the negative time in your day when nothing on your to-do list gets done. Your brain and several other systems in your body see it quite differently. "Your brain is very active during sleep doing important things — it's not just resting. Physiologically sleep is defined as a state our bodies enter into during which brain wave activity changes and our nervous system is less reactive to external stimuli (i.e. we temporarily leave consciousness). But our sleep is not constant throughout the night. We cycle through four distinct sleep phases multiple times (five if you count "awake" as one stage).
There are two stages of light sleep. The lightest is the stage of sleep you're likely in if you nod off during a lecture when consciousness is decreased, but the brain is still processing some information around you (sometimes hearing your name or another stimulus will jolt you awake). Intermediate light sleep is slightly deeper, which is harder to awaken from.
Deep slow-wave sleep is the next stage of sleep. This is the deepest, most restful, and most restorative stage of sleep when it's hardest to awaken. If you do get woken up during this stage of sleep you're likely to feel groggy. And finally, there's REM sleep (short for "rapid eye movement sleep"), which is when we dream. Our bodies tend to spend more time in restful slow wave sleep earlier in the night when our bodies and minds are most tired. Later in the night, we tend to spend more time in REM sleep. There are important electrical and chemical processes that happen in the brain and throughout the body during all the stages of sleep. Here's how they affect our health:

Sleep is the prime time for learning and memory

One of the most active parts of the body during sleep is the brain, Bazil says. There are pronounced changes in the electrical activity of the brain during sleep, which the evidence suggests is a result of the brain's trillions of nerve cells rewiring themselves. This rewiring, which happens during deep, slow-wave sleep, is how we process and are thus able to retain new information we may have learned throughout the day, Bazil explains. "Your brain is making a map of the information," he says — "making new connections and breaking other ones."

That means skipping sleep to cram for an exam or important presentation isn't doing you any favors, Bazil says. The evidence suggests that if you spend all night trying to learn something new and miss a few hours of sleep to do so, your brain's not going to retain that information the same way it would have if you'd gotten a full night of sleep, he says. "Your brain needs to process that information, which you only do when you're asleep."

Sleep also helps keep our attention and focus sharp, Bazil adds. We all (likely) know the "fuzzy" feeling that results after a night of too little sleep, especially if you're trying to pay attention to a lecture on a complicated topic or focus on a complex task. But it's also important to note that chronic sleep debt accumulates and research shows the attention and focus deficits caused by sleep loss accumulate over time

if you spend all night trying to learn something new and miss a few hours of sleep to do so, your brain's not going to retain that information the same way it would have if you'd gotten a full night of sleep.

Poor sleep makes you moody

Think cranky toddler in need of a nap. We all know that sleep (and lack of it) affects mood and irritability. But brain-imaging studies have shown that a good night's sleep helps our brain regulate mood and cope with whatever the next day brings. Conversely, insufficient sleep boosts a part of the brain that's known to be affected by depression, anxiety, and other psychiatric disorders.

Without sleep, the brain had reverted to more primitive patterns of activity — in that it was unable to put emotional experiences into context and produced controlled appropriate responses.

Chronic insomnia has also been linked to an increased risk of developing a mood disorder, including anxiety or depression. Another study found that after a week of getting just four-and-a-half hours of sleep per night, individuals reported worse moods (in terms of feeling stressed, angry, sad, or mentally exhausted).

Not getting sleep can make you sick

Outside of the brain, there's a lot of changing throughout the rest of the body during sleep, too. Our heart rate and body temperatures drop, our breathing rate slightly decreases and becomes very regular (at least during most stages of sleep), and kidney function slows down (which is why you typically don't feel the urge to pee as frequently during sleep as when you're awake).

And at the same time, other systems in the body ramp way up during sleep. There's an increase in the release of growth hormones during sleep (this is when kids get taller, our skin cells regenerate, and our hair gets longer), as well as the hormones that regulate appetite. Sleep is also when our muscles repair damage (and regular wear and tear) throughout the day.

Sleep also plays an integral role in regulating the body's immune system, which is responsible for fighting off all sorts of problems from the common cold to more serious chronic problems like cancer. Studies have shown that individuals are more likely to catch a cold virus when they're sleep-deprived and that vaccines can be less effective after a poor night of sleep.

And thanks to all these important roles that sleep plays in the body, chronically getting poor sleep can have some pretty serious consequences. Cutting sleep short by even just two to three hours a night over time has been linked to an increased risk of obesity, diabetes, cardiovascular disease, hypertension, and premature death.

5. Your vision trumps all other senses

Despite being one of our five main senses, vision seems to take precedence over the others:

Hear a piece of information, and three days later you'll remember 10 percent of it. Add a picture and you'll remember 65 percent.

Pictures beat text as well, in part because reading is so inefficient for us. Our brain sees words as lots of tiny pictures, and we have to identify certain features in the letters to be able to read them. That takes time.

Not only is it surprising that we rely on our vision so much, but it isn't even that good! Take this fact, for instance:

Our brain is doing all this guessing because it doesn't know where things are. In a three-dimensional world, the light falls on our retina in a two-dimensional fashion. So our brain approximates viewable images.

Let's look at this image. It shows you how much of your brain is dedicated just to vision and how it affects other parts of the brain. It's a truly staggering amount, compared to any other area:

6. Introversion and extroversion come from different wiring in the brain

I just recently realized that introversion and extroversion are not related to how outgoing or shy we are, but rather how our brains recharge.

Here's how the brains of introverts and extroverts differ:

Research has found that there is a difference in the brains of extroverted and introverted people in terms of how we process rewards and how our genetic makeup differs. Extroverts, their brains respond more strongly when a gamble pays off. Part of this is simply genetic, but it's partly the difference in their dopamine systems as well.

An experiment that had people take gambles while in a brain scanner found the following:

When the gambles they took paid off, the more extroverted group showed a stronger response in two crucial brain regions: the amygdala and the nucleus accumbens.

The nucleus accumbens is part of the dopamine system, which affects how we learn, and is generally known for motivating us to search for rewards. The difference in the dopamine system in the extrovert's brain tends to push them towards seeking out novelty, taking risks, and enjoying unfamiliar or surprising situations more than others. The amygdala is responsible for processing emotional stimuli, which gives extroverts that rush of excitement when they try something highly stimulating which might overwhelm an introvert.

More research has shown that the difference comes from how introverts and extroverts process stimuli. That is, the stimulation coming into our brains is processed differently depending on our personality. For extroverts, the pathway is much shorter. It runs through an area where taste, touch, and visual and auditory sensory processing takes place. For introverts, stimuli run through a long, complicated pathway in areas of the brain associated with remembering, planning, and solving problems.

7. We tend to like people who make mistakes more

Making mistakes makes us more likable, due to something called the Pratfall Effect.
What is the Pratfall Effect?
Have you ever made an embarrassing mistake in public? Do you think it affected how much other people liked you or how competent they thought you were? The Pratfall Effect is a surprising twist on how peoples' opinions of us can change after making an error (and it applies to brands and products too).

8. Meditation can rewire your brain for the better

Here's another one that surprised me. I thought meditation was only good for improving focus and helping me to stay calm throughout the day, but it has a whole bunch of great benefits.

Here are a few examples:

Less anxiety

This point is pretty technical, but it's really interesting. The more we meditate, the less anxiety we have, and it turns out this is because we're loosening the connections of particular neural pathways. This sounds bad, but it's not.

What happens without meditation is that there's a section of our brains that's sometimes called the Me Center (it's technically the medial prefrontal cortex). This is the part that processes information relating to ourselves and our experiences. Normally the neural pathways from the bodily sensation and fear centers of the brain to the Me Center are really strong. When you experience a scary or upsetting sensation, it triggers a strong reaction in your Me Center, making you feel scared and under attack.

Here is how anxiety and agitation decrease with just a 20-minute meditation session: When we meditate, especially when we are just getting started with meditation, we weaken this neural connection. This means that we don't react as strongly to sensations that might have once lit up our Me Centers. As we weaken this connection, we simultaneously strengthen the connection between what's known as our Assessment Center (the part of our brains known for reasoning) and our bodily sensation and fear centers. So when we experience scary or upsetting sensations, we can more easily look at them rationally. Here's a good example:

For example, when you experience pain, rather than becoming anxious and assuming it means something is wrong with you, you can watch the pain rise and fall without becoming ensnared in a story about what it might mean.

9. Exercise can reorganize the brain and boost your willpower

Sure, exercise is good for your body, but what about your brain? Well, there's a link between exercise and mental alertness, in a similar way that happiness and exercise are related.

A lifetime of exercise can result in a sometimes astonishing elevation in cognitive performance, compared with those who are sedentary. Exercisers outperform couch potatoes in tests that measure long-term memory, reasoning, attention, problem-solving and even so-called fluid-intelligence tasks.

Of course, exercise can also make us happier, as we've explored before:

If you start exercising, your brain recognizes this as a moment of stress. As your heart pressure increases, the brain thinks you are either fighting the enemy or fleeing from it. To protect yourself and your brain from stress, you release a protein called BDNF

(Brain-Derived Neurotrophic Factor). This BDNF has a protective and also reparative element to your memory neurons and acts as a reset switch. That's why we often feel so at ease and things are clear after exercising and eventually happy.
At the same time, endorphins, another chemical to fight stress, are released in your brain.

10. You can make your brain think time is going slowly by doing new things
Ever wished you didn't find yourself saying "Where does the time go!" every June when you realize the year is half over? This is a neat trick that relates to how our brains perceive time. Once you know how it works, you can trick your brain into thinking time is moving more slowly.
Essentially, our brains take a whole bunch of information from our senses and organize it in a way that makes sense to us, before we ever perceive it. So what we think is our sense of time is just a whole bunch of information presented to us in a particular way, as determined by our brains:
When our brains receive new information, it doesn't necessarily come in the proper order. This information needs to be reorganized and presented to us in a form we understand. When familiar information is processed, this doesn't take much time at all. New information, however, is a bit slower and makes time feel elongated.
Even stranger, it isn't just a single area of the brain that controls our time perception—it's done by a whole bunch of brain areas, unlike our common five senses, which can each be pinpointed to a single, specific area.
When we receive lots of new information, it takes our brains a while to process it all. The longer this processing takes, the longer that period feels:
When we're in life-threatening situations, for instance, "we remember the time as longer because we record more of the experience. Life-threatening experiences make us pay attention, but we don't gain superhuman powers of perception."
The same thing happens when we hear enjoyable music, because "greater attention leads to the perception of a longer period."
Conversely, if your brain doesn't have to process lots of new information, time seems to move faster, so the same amount of time will feel shorter than it would otherwise. This happens when you take in lots of information that's familiar because you've processed it before. Your brain doesn't have to work very hard, so it processes time faster.

What is peace of mind?
The phrase peace of mind is about a sense of tranquility and confidence, where our mental balance is in accord with universal understanding. In short, it means that we have within ourselves the tools to deal with adversity. Thus, this ability occurs through mind control, where the effects of any external factors such as stress are also blocked.

How to achieve peace of mind
1. Think positive

At many times in your daily life, you live a situation, but your mind is far away thinking of other things. This is one of the main problems that make people feel restless and even stressed out. You cannot have inner peace if you don't have your head in order. The way you think has a lot to do with the preoccupations you have every day. If you are pessimistic all the time, you are conditioning yourself to have a bad day, and things go wrong. Every time you have a negative thought, correct yourself immediately and see the bright side of the situation. Move your mind to a more positive mental state.

2. Practice meditation

Guided meditation stimulates creativity and opens the doors to solve problems in ways that you would not have thought of before. This act of concentration can bring many benefits of meditation into your life, as well as helping you cope better with your responsibility. Also, meditation prevents stress from taking over you. The best thing is that it is so simple to learn, and anyone can put it into practice at home. Once you are encouraged to try this good habit, you will never want to leave it, and you will feel much calmer inwardly. You can watch meditation videos about peace on YouTube.

3. Let things go

For the sake of your mental health, letting things go will allow you to have peace of mind. Life isn't always fair. Sometimes, bad things happen to us, even though we've done nothing wrong. We could spend our whole lives getting revenge for all the injustices that happen to us, but then we also wouldn't have peace of mind. Finding peace isn't about being passive about what happens to us. It's more so about having the self-control to not let it take over our thoughts and actions. Accepting an injustice, such as a dismissal of a job, will allow you to plan for your next chapter, interview, and job.

4. Focus on the present

If you want a peaceful mind, live in the present. When we have negative thoughts in our mind, we get stuck in the past. We'll replay bad memories and painful situations. When we have anxious thoughts in our mind, it's because we're fearing the future. However, when we have happy thoughts, it's because we're living in the present. Pop culture glamorizes anxiety and depression in a lot of ways. The tabloids regularly cover people's mental health breakdowns. What they don't cover often, are people who have peace of mind and simply enjoy life. You can find peace by getting out of your head and experiencing the real world.

5. Accept what you can't change

Acceptance is all about controlling what you can but accepting what you can't control. There are billions of people in the world. Everyone has their own agenda, goals, wants, and needs. Your mental state will collapse if you're always trying to control the uncontrollable. You can have peace of mind by understanding that sometimes things are outside of our control. Take ownership of what you can, such as your behaviour and attitude. However, accept the things you can't like ruminating thoughts, other people, natural disasters, time, and so on. You can do everything in your power to prevent something from happening, but when the

6. Read at least twenty minutes a day

Reading is one of the best gifts of peace of mind you can give your brain. This is because it is not only an interesting hobby but also relaxes and gives you a greater capacity for concentration and reasoning. Don't complain that you don't have time to read a complete book. You only need to spend twenty minutes of your day reading a little to begin your finding peace journey. In this way, you will realize that it is not so difficult, but also entertaining and a great help. Don't let your anxiety destroy your **morning routine**. If you want to have peace of mind, consider reading books about how the brain works, meditation, mindfulness, or other positive topics. There's plenty of **meditation books** out there from you to choose from that will give you peace of mind.

7. Spend some time alone

Your well being will greatly improve when you spend some time alone. While it's important to build social connections with others, most of the time, our peace of mind is disrupted by others. When things get a little too chaotic and you can't get a minute's peace, consider removing your worry by isolating yourself temporarily. Being alone every now and then can be great for your health, happiness, and inner peace. Experiencing the mental freedom of being alone will allow you to recharge your batteries, build yourself back up, and move forward. Before you do this, tell other people where you'll be so they don't worry. For example, some people might choose to take a one or two-week vacation alone to pull themselves together. Sometimes, a little break will give your mind peace and the feeling that you can solve your problem.

8. Relax your expectations

Life never follows the path you have outlined in your plans. Many times we spend too much time thinking about how things are going to be in our future. But when reality does not meet our expectations, we get frustrated quickly. The truth is that what you need will come in the form of what you expect from life. The best thing is to go through those difficult moments without seeing the problems.

Remember that if things don't go as planned, it does not mean that they are not taking you along the path you need. Always look for the lesson of each situation and don't let these "detours" steal your peace of mind. Learn to accept reality and the part of it that you cannot change. That is the best starting point for you to discover the ones that you can modify and how to do it.

9. Speak with a therapist

Finding a therapist to speak with once a month can help you have peace of mind. A therapist can improve your well being by giving you the tools you need to manage ruminating thoughts, promote calmness, and embrace yourself. Rest assured, seeing a therapist is good for your mental health. It can be really healthy to have a sounding board to prevent your thoughts from destroying your peace of mind. Challenge any preconceived notions of what it means to see a therapist as it can bring you joy and sign you up for success.

10. Exercise

Create an exercise routine when you want peace of mind. While exercise can feel like the opposite thing you feel like doing when stressed, it can bring about a sense of calm and relaxation. Running can make you feel free while pumping you up with feel-good endorphins to help calm the mind. **Challenge yourself** to exercise at least four days a week or by setting a goal of 10,000 steps a day. Any distress you feel will vanish when moving your body. Exercise is like free therapy. So test yourself to push harder and fight the urge to sit back.

11. Give yourself time

Resilience is not a speed competition, take all the time you need to **overcome adversity** and take on the necessary learning. Healing **emotional pain** is a complex process, and like all, it is best concluded without unnecessary haste. Do not be pressured to take the lessons and do not allow others to place excessive expectations on you to move forward. Overcoming some things is not a matter of a couple of days, it takes a lot of effort and learning to feel good again.

Live the moment to find peace of mind, and see one step at a time. Keep in mind that not because yesterday was a particularly painful day, it will be to even today. Not because today is a difficult day, every day will be the same. If you break, then get up and keep walking. Nothing happens because it is hard for you to move on or because the strength fails. Explore your pain, recognize it, and work on it to overcome difficulties.

12. Do daily acts of kindness

The easiest way to have peace of mind is by doing **acts of kindness** daily. Every day choose to do a **good deed** for another person. You could write a kind comment on a Facebook post, call a loved one to tell them why you love them and are grateful for them, or write an article with ideas that'll help someone in distress. There are millions of kind gestures you can do. When someone hurts you, recognize that they're in pain, instead of evil or mean-spirited. And in response, do something kind for them too. You can send a note or call them on the phone to tell them why you love them despite how they've hurt you.

13. Get some extra sleep

It's easier to have peace of mind when you're well-rested. Those who only sleep a few hours each night are more likely to have racing thoughts, anxiety, and even depression. Sleep allows you to process the day's information subconsciously. When you sleep a full eight hours each night, your brain is likely calmer so it's easier to deal with the personal issues that arises during difficult periods. A **calm mind** means that you'll be able to handle difficult situations with kindness and grace. So, aim to get some shut eye each night by going to bed a bit earlier to wake up with peace of mind.

14. Open your feelings with someone you trust

Being **mentally strong** does not mean not having feelings, but knowing how to handle them. It is natural that in the face of adversity, you **feel overwhelmed** and crying. Keeping your pain or worry can plunge you into isolation that causes you a sense of loneliness and even depression. Your friends, family, and loved ones are there to support and accompany you even in the most challenging parts of your life. Go to them when you need them. Having someone you trust at your side will help you channel those emotions to leave your **mind and body** more easily.

15. Take a walk

We are part of nature, and that is why being in it is so good. Even if you live in a large city, you can find ways to maintain that contact, such as in parks, or some green area. Try to **include this kind of walk** in your routine, step on the grass, touch trees, enjoy this powerful connection, and recharge your batteries to gain some peace of mind. Another thing you can also do is go rollerblading or cycling. The idea is to take a quiet walk without interruptions and enjoy it to the fullest.

16. Listen to classical or ambient music

The power of sound within the mind is incredible, to such an extent that certain songs calm us and make us feel happy. The classic compositions are the most recommended to stimulate the brain, increasing its ability to concentrate and study. They also provide immense calm to the body. **Ambient sounds** that mimic nature are another very effective alternative with which you can try. Especially when you are meditating, taking a walk, or doing something artistic. You can also listen to **positive songs** that uplift you.

17. Practice Gratitude

Writing a **gratitude list** will help you reduce the feeling of stress by reminding you of all the good things you have in your life. Every day, think about the things you're grateful for having. Or write down good things that happened to you that day that you feel grateful for. You could be grateful for having specific people in your life or certain opportunities. The phrase, "I'm grateful for..." should be in your regular vocabulary when interacting with others. Let people know you **appreciate them**. Test yourself by writing down your gratitude list without looking at other people's lists. Then, look at other people's lists and compare what you have that you completely didn't realize.

18. Avoid comparing yourself to others

Stop comparing yourself to others if you want to have peace of mind. You'll have greater peace by focusing on comparing yourself today to who you were than by comparing yourself to someone else. The feeling of insecurity vanishes when the comparison game is only played with yourself. Strive to become a better version of yourself, but don't beat yourself up for not being that person yet. There's no need to wonder **"what is wrong with me?"** or **"why am I not good enough?"** Instead, ask yourself, "what would the future me do to have peace of mind?" and then start building those traits into your life.

19. Look at things from a different perspective

Sometimes, physical or temporal distance is all you need to see more clearly and better understand problems. Regardless of the problem that comes your way, always be clear about the good and positive things you have as a person. A very real part of you exists independently of your immediate concerns, problems, and frustrations. If you **feel overwhelmed**, step back, and observe the way you experience things. Your body may feel pain, but that does not define you. Eventually, that pain will dissipate and leave you learning.

20. Love and practice self care

Always remember to **love yourself**, treat yourself with love, **forgive yourself**, and finally **treat yourself the same way you treat a loved one**. When you love and respect yourself, life becomes lighter because you no longer charge yourself with unreachable perfection. You see yourself more humanely and kindly.

21. Prepare for rainy days

You can help yourself have peace of mind by preparing for rainy days. In life, curveballs will always happen, such as sudden job loss, death of a loved one, or an unexpected big expense. You can prepare for these rainy days in so many ways. For example, if you save up in an emergency fund or build out your income streams, you'll be prepared for unexpected job losses or big expenses. Telling loved ones how much you appreciate them while they're alive will prevent any guilt you may feel from an unexpected death. You can have greater peace by having open conversations with people and planning ahead.

Every day is a new beginning and a new opportunity to improve things and keep growing. Do not focus on the past or what it could be, but work to improve your future prospects and gain greater learning. Keep your mind at peace, and remember that the world does not end with problems. Every day you have the opportunity to recalculate your course if necessary. Learning to interpret difficulties and not clinging to frustration takes time. It's up to you to decide how you want to deal with problems. When we realize this, it's actually more empowering than frightening, bringing more peace of mind to our life.

Subconscious Mind Power Explained

Your subconscious mind is like a huge memory bank. It permanently stores everything that ever happens to you, and its capacity is virtually unlimited.

By the time you reach the age of 21, you've already permanently stored more than one hundred times the contents of the entire generation.

Under hypnosis, people can often remember, with perfect clarity, past events that happened many years before.

But why don't we actively recall everything our subconscious minds hold?

While your unconscious memory is virtually perfect, it is your conscious recall that is suspect.

The exciting news is we can use our conscious minds to reprogram our subconscious minds and harness the power of positive thinking to overcome negative thoughts and bad habits to achieve all of our life dreams.

Let me show you how.

What Is Your Conscious Mind VS Your Subconscious Mind?

The conscious mind can be described as whatever you are currently aware of. What you are feeling, doing, seeing, touching, experiencing. You are conscious of it or aware of it. Consciousness does not involve stored information. It is what is happening now. It does involve thinking and making decisions. It is easy to control your conscious mind because you can use it to make choices.

In contrast, your subconscious mind is always working in the background, but you are not necessarily aware of it. Sometimes called the unconscious mind, your subconscious mind contains all of the stored information of everything you have ever experienced. Because of this, it influences how you react to things, such as why you are shy, lazy, eat too much, or have an addiction. On the positive side, your subconscious mind also affects things like why you are motivated, confident, successful, cheerful, hopeful, and so on.

The key is using your consciousness to positively influence your subconscious thoughts. Learning how to use the two together is a powerful tool.

How Your Subconscious Mind Operates

Every moment that you are awake, your five senses are taking in a constant stream of information. These experiences are stored as memories, like a computer stores data. But we do not need to actively recall most of this information. We probably forget 95-99% of our daily activities.

However, we know these thoughts and images are still in your brain because hypnosis can bring back deep memories.

Studies in the field of psychology on how the brain works indicate that the experiences we have shape the way we think and act, especially experiences in our early childhood. Although you do not remember most of your life data, the unconscious data in your head influence 90 to 95% of your behavior.

Your subconscious mind can be compared to flying a plane on autopilot. It is constantly running programs to control how we walk, sit, breathe, talk, and so on. We don't have to think about these things, they just happen because the information to do them is stored in your brain.

Your subconscious mind has what is called a homeostatic impulse. It keeps your body temperature at 98.6 degrees Fahrenheit, just as it keeps you breathing regularly and keeps your heart beating at a certain rate.

Through your autonomic nervous system, it maintains a balance among the hundreds of chemicals in your billions of cells so that your entire physical machine functions in complete harmony most of the time.

Your subconscious mind also practices homeostasis in your mental realm, by keeping you thinking and acting in a manner consistent with what you have done and said in the past.

Your subconscious mind causes you to feel emotionally and physically uncomfortable whenever you attempt to do anything new or different or to change any of your established patterns of behavior. The sense of fear and discomfort are psychological signs that your subconscious has been activated. But it's been working to establish those behavior patterns in the background long before you'll ever notice such feelings.

The tendency to commit to these patterns is one reason why habits can be so hard to break. However, when you learn to purposefully create such patterns, you can harness the power of habit and purposefully instill new comfort zones to which your subconscious will adapt.

You can feel your subconscious pulling you back toward your comfort zone each time you try something new. Even thinking about doing something different from what you're accustomed to will make you feel tense and uneasy.

This is why forming new habits that will help you reach your goals, such as following time management tips, may be tougher to implement at first, but once they become habit or routine they will stay in your comfort zone. In doing so, you've reprogrammed your subconscious to work in your favor.

Changing Habits: Using Your Conscious Mind To Properly Program Your Subconscious Mind

Since your subconscious mind has such a great amount of control over your positive and negative behaviors, the key is to train your brain to produce more positive behaviors. This is where your conscious mind comes in. You can use your consciousness to reprogram or retrain your subconscious mind to do things that are more beneficial to your world now and for your future.

Do you have goals you want to reach, habits that seem impossible to overcome, hopes for a dream job that would change your life, or a vision of the future that looks very different from today?

Using your conscious thoughts to program your subconscious mind can bring you success in all areas of your life that you are looking for.

It starts by following these four steps:

1. Recognize The Roadblock

First, you need to identify what is holding you back from achieving what you want to achieve.

What are your limiting thoughts or fears?

For example, if you desire to write a book, but you just can't seem to get started or finish, what is keeping you from doing that? Do you think no one will read it or you don't have enough time or you're not a trained writer?

All of these thoughts are what you imagine to be true, but they are not necessarily true. Your unconscious mind has been programmed to respond that way, and your conscious choices will follow.

Roadblocks can also be physical barriers. Perhaps you want to lose weight, but you allow your habit of scrolling through social media for 30 minutes a day to fill the time that could be spent exercising.

Think about your goals and dreams and find out what thoughts, habits, ideas, or barriers are keeping you from achieving them.

2. Let Go Of Limiting Thoughts

Once you know what your limiting thoughts are, accept them, embrace them, and then let them go.

Sometimes this requires you to bring pain to the surface, into your conscious mind, so you can face it and then release it.

Perhaps you struggle with the ability to develop a trusting relationship, for example, but you realize you did not have that modeled for you in your childhood. When you understand what is causing your emotions, you can address them and find a better way to respond.

3. Set Up The Intention With Your Conscious Mind

Now it is time to unleash the power of positive thinking and reprogram your subconscious.

Your conscious thoughts and actions can reprogram your subconscious mind in heartbeat. A positive message can reprogram how you feel, heal trauma, and change habits that make your lives stagnant to blossom into fulfilling lives that focus on the things that matter most.

Use your conscious mind to set an expectation of what will happen in your life.

For example, when faced with your roadblock, say to yourself, "Even though I've done this in the past, I no longer do it now."

Your subconscious mind will listen, just as it has listened to all of the other input it has ever received. Over time, your subconscious mind has no choice but to follow. It is no longer interested in old habits because it has found a new habit.

The key is visualizing what you want to happen, having a plan for how you will react to your roadblocks, using your conscious mind to stay aware and recognize what's going on, and choosing to follow your plan at the moment.

4. Let Your Subconscious Mind Take Over

The point is to eventually allow your conscious to relax and let your subconscious take over. Once you have given your unconscious the other way to respond, it will assume that is the way it should respond.

With the right word, action, or idea, you have created a new way for your subconscious mind to search its databanks and find a positive, uplifting, and empowering way to respond.

Positive Tools to Help You Tap Into Your Subconscious Mind

There are many things you can do to reprogram your subconscious mind daily. Be proactive by incorporating them into your routine. Here are some of the most successful ways to harness the power of your subconscious mind with your conscious efforts.

Positive Affirmations

Your subconscious mind makes everything you say and do fit a pattern consistent with your self-concept, your "master program."

This is why repeating positive affirmations are so effective — you can reprogram your thought patterns by slipping in positive and success-oriented sound bites.

Start every day with a positive affirmation. Say one each time you are faced with a roadblock or challenge.

Inspirational Quotes

Reading inspirational quotes is so impactful for people committed to positive thinking. By focusing your thoughts on uplifting words and ideas, your subconscious will begin to implement a positive pattern in your way of thinking and your outlook on life.

Apply the same principle by reading an uplifting article each day, reading helpful books relevant to your life goals, listening to educational or inspirational podcasts, and watching a motivational video or film.

SMART Goals

All your habits of thinking and acting are stored in your subconscious mind. It has memorized all your comfort zones and it works to keep you in them. This is why it's so important to make writing SMART goals a regular habit. Over time, staying productive and focusing on all of your goals will become part of your comfort zone.

Power of Positive Thinking

Your subconscious mind is subjective. It does not think or reason independently; it merely obeys the commands it receives from your conscious mind.

Just as your conscious mind can be thought of as the gardener planting seeds, your subconscious mind can be thought of as the garden, or fertile soil, in which the seeds germinate and grow.

This is why harnessing the power of positive thinking is important to the foundation of your entire thought process. Your conscious mind *commands* and your subconscious mind *obey*.

Consciously choose to feed your subconscious with positive, empowering thoughts.

Habits of Highly Successful People

For those looking to expand their realm of comfort zones, I highly recommend considering the habits of successful people as they are the patterns commonly adopted by the minds of great leaders and thinkers. Unlocking the power of these behaviors will put you one step closer to being able to make the same things happen in your life. These habits include planning your day the night before, numbering your priorities on your to-do list, and completing your most important task first.

Train Your Subconscious Mind to Create Your Best Life

Learning techniques to reprogram your subconscious mind will help you believe in yourself because your confidence will no longer be challenged by fear of the unknown. But more importantly, doing so will train your brain to be in line with your true desires, dreams, and life goals.

The more in tune with your subconscious you become, the closer you will be to breaking through to success. To help you get started right now, download a free copy of my Personal Development Plan Template.

Chapter 2: The Power of Words

There always has and will be a power in words, but when a combination of vocals and a distinct instrumental is harmonized, it has the potential to transcend the power of words alone. Music can be interpreted by the listener through the perception of the individual. The perception of the individual is what gives human beings the ability to create the imaginative design by combining things in one's mind or interpreting the reality he or she faces on earth. For instance, let's state that an individual listens to a song he or she takes a strong liking to. This individual has the power to use his or her imaginative design to reconstruct the song he or she is listening to and gear it toward a completely unrelated topic, not about the song's content. An explanation for a thought process of this nature is that the presentation of the song led the individual to feel empathic about the vocal and instrumental emotional appeal. The way something is said or how something sounds has the ability for humans to take their interpretation of what's happily presented, sadly presented, angrily presented, etc., and relate their interpretation to a mental image, a person, a situation, an event, etc.

The Scary Power of Negative Words

How the Words We Choose Shape Our Lives

Words have power. Their meaning crystallizes perceptions that shape our beliefs, drive our behavior, and ultimately, create our world. Their power arises from our emotional responses when we read, speak, or hear them. Just say the word "fire" while barbequing, in the workplace, or a crowded theater, and you'll get three completely different but powerful emotional and energetic reactions.

The Illusion of Life

Quantum physics long ago determined that physical matter doesn't exist, that everything is just energy in different states of vibration. "Atoms or elementary particles themselves are not real; they form a world of potentialities or possibilities, rather than one of things or facts." This energy vibrates at an infinite number of subtle frequencies that cause it to appear as all the different creations we see in our world. There has been a great deal of research in recent years as to whether the universe we live in is a holographic experience, and it seems that this is very close to the truth.

And so, it seems life is more of an energy flow than a collection of solid things. What that means for us is that if we stay conscious of the energy we contain, based on the emotions we feel, we can make deliberate choices that alter our frequency and create the realities we desire. If we're feeling down about something, we can choose to reframe the situation and raise our spirits. With a renewed perspective and a higher, more positive energetic vibration, we stand a much better chance of bringing good into our lives, rather than bitterly repeating old mistakes.

Words are extremely powerful tools that we can use to uplift our energy and improve our lives, though we're often not conscious of the words we speak, read, and expose ourselves to. Yes, even the words of others can easily affect our vibration. Spend a few minutes with a chronic complainer who uses all sorts of negative terms, and you'll feel your energy bottom out. Words have great power, so choose them (and your friends) wisely!

Throw-away Words

How many times a day do we throw our words away? We say things like, "I hate my hair," "I'm so stupid," and "I'm such a klutz." We never think that these words bring negative energy into our vibration and affect us on a physical level, but they do. Experiments were conducted with water. Why? Because sound vibration travels through water four times faster than it does through open air. Consider the fact that your body is over 70% water and you'll understand how quickly the vibration from negative words resonates in your cells. Ancient scriptures tell us that life and death are in the power of the tongue. As it turns out, that's not a metaphor.

How words can help

1. Making Words Work.
To consciously harness the power of words for your benefit, start with the ones you're using.

2. No Name-Calling or Self-Criticism.
Everyone is doing the best they can at any moment in time with the consciousness they have to work with, including you. Be kind and offer yourself the same empathy and compassion you'd extend to anyone else.

3. Stop All Self-Deprecation.
Never make your body, something you've accomplished, or anything else in your life the butt of a joke. Words have power, and quantum energy doesn't have a sense of humor.

4. Resist Gossiping and Speaking Ill of Others.
Your words can't resonate in anyone else's body but your own.

5. Go on a Negativity Diet.
Instead of saying that a meal was terrible say, "I've had better." You've said what you wanted to say without putting negative energy through your body—you even used a positive word to do it!

6. Boost the Positive Energy of Words.
Instead of saying something like you had a good time at a concert, ramp up the positive energy by saying great, terrific, or fantastic, instead. These feel much better and generate a bigger energetic response in the body.

7. If you have some negative nancy in your circle of friends,
limit the time you spend with them or find better friends. Negative energy has a way of dragging everything surrounding it in, like a big black hole. Avoid it when you can.

8. Surround yourself with positive, uplifting words.
Put affirmations on sticky notes around your home and office that say wonderful things about you, your family, or your goals. Wear clothes that have positive messages or phrases on them. Imagine the kind of positive energy you'll be generating for yourself when you're wearing positivity all day long. As you keep doing these things, you use the power of repetition in a highly effective way for your benefit. You have the power to change your world, and using words consciously is one of the quickest ways to shift the energy you bring into your life.

The Power of Words – You Become What You Say

The power of words has often become debated as to how they can affect our lives. Most successful people tend to agree with the idea that you become what you say. Your words are a deeper reflection of what is going on inside your head. If you speak words of success and praise of yourself you tend to become just that. We will take a look at how words influence who we are.

Blessing or Condemnation – The words you speak can be a blessing to yourself or a condemning attitude that may hinder achieving goals in life. The power of words lies not just in their sounds and syllables but in the emotions that they conjure in your life. When you speak down upon yourself and talk of how you are not good or you will never be rich you draw emotions of despair. You then condemn yourself to a life of poverty and low self-esteem because this is what you allow yourself to believe. Those who have prospered and done amazing things for themselves had an amazing skill of never giving up. This does not come easy because life tends to knock people to their knees. Those who tell themselves they are defeated will quit while those who only tell themselves positive things are more likely to keep moving forward when they are taking the hits from life. Every person can choose what they tell themselves so it is in every person's best interest to let themselves know they can win and have good things in their lives.

Encourage Yourself – We all know that words have the power to dishearten or can conjure extreme enthusiasm about something. If you have the talents and desire to accomplish something in your life then start by using powerful words and images that spark motivation. Remind yourself of the victories that you have experienced and you came out on top. Then remind yourself with words of how great you are at something or how determined you are. The best way to use words is when you mix them with emotions and let them spark enthusiasm in you for something great. Words alone have power and when you mix them with power visualizations they become a deadly weapon. They can either be good or bad depending on what you want. Those who are miserable tend to dwell only on disheartening words and always bring up past failures. This produces low self-esteem and is toxic to your morale. Meanwhile, a person of happiness blocks past failures after the lesson has been learned. Rather, they dwell on the success they have enjoyed in life and remind themselves of how worthy they are of something. This equals the most powerful emotion a human can have: UNCONDITIONAL love for yourself. If you can achieve this then there is nothing within your skill level that is not obtainable.

In Conclusion – The power of words can prove to be very destructive or very motivating depending on what you want them to have. If you remove all limiting and damaging words from your vocabulary and head and move to a more positive place you can become your best friend. Choose your words carefully because they tend to become reality.

Words are powerful. Spoken, written, or simply the words we use in our minds — all words have potential power.

What's powerful about words?

 Why does our linguistic ability help to define us in the scope of our abilities and potential? How can we use words and their power to our advantage?

The choices we make with our language set the parameters for our lives. The skill of expression we possess can contribute to many facets of our ability to succeed personally and professionally. The real power in words is their meaning and interpretation. That is also the real power in life.

Determining the meaning of events in our lives, and our responsibility to choose to find an empowering meaning are some of the most important things we can ever grasp. If we choose a disempowering meaning that is our choice. When something happens to us, we can consciously control our verdict on the positive or negative meaning behind it. Our first reactions to something aren't always conscious, but then we can step in and reframe the meaning.

For example, let's say you failed a test. Does this mean that you're a failure? Or does this mean that you now know areas you need to work on to improve? That's up to us to determine, and even if we feel like a failure initially — we can step in and transform what the failure means to us internally. We can cultivate a positive interpretation of nearly all events in our lives.

Some call it looking for the silver lining or relentless optimism. How does this have anything to do with the power of words?

Words can often have more than one meaning, just like failing a test. However, words do not have the dynamic range and malleability that our interpretation of life does. The definition of a cat is different than the definition of a dog, and no rose-colored glasses can change that. So, we have more leeway to determine an empowering meaning from events, than we do from words. Ugly means ugly, ugly does not mean pretty.

The power of words comes into play during the times when we define our reality. The words we use in our minds repeatedly to describe ourselves and our identity are some of the most powerful forces in our lives.

If we constantly utter self-deprecating language in our internal dialogue, we are allowing the power of words to work against us. Telling ourselves that we are fat, weak, worthless, or stupid can sap us of our power to find positive meaning from our experiences. If we tell ourselves we're stupid all day, then when we fail a test we can seldom see the perspective that it may have a silver lining. We are much more likely to use it to affirm our belief that we are stupid. "See, I failed. I *am* stupid."

The emotions we feel, the events we experience, and our ability to interact with other humans is all controlled by language. If we want more control, and more agency in our lives we can start with a greater understanding of the potential power in what we say to ourselves and others.

Some of the power comes from the words themselves, and some come from the emotion and intensity with which we use them. If we say to someone "I hate you" in a playful tone, with a smile and laugh — we can be sure to receive a different reaction than if we shout it at the top of our lungs in an aggressive tone.

Our words are also filtered by those who hear them and based on their psycho-emotional state they can interpret their meanings far differently than we intended. This is especially true of text messaging. Everyone has read a text message from someone and interpreted it wrong based on their present disposition when they read it.

All of us know that sometimes we tend to read too deeply through the words of a text message and search for an emotional revelation or justification. We read "cool" but it can take on any meaning we like. Cool could mean it's not cool. Cool could mean stop talking to me. Cool could mean a lot, just like failing a test.

So be careful about going too deep in the search for words' meanings without having the added benefits of hearing tone, seeing facial expressions, and interpreting body language. Be aware that the power of words works both ways — power in their utterance, and power in their ingestion.

When we speak, write, think, or otherwise use words we are engaged in something we should be mindful of. The power of words in our world is undeniable. Our linguistic ability can set us on a trajectory to achieve great things or to remain disenchanted with our lives.

Moment by moment we are interacting with ourselves and others using language. We take what we know from our upbringing, what we regularly see and hear in our lives, and the words from the media we ingest and it becomes how we can express ourselves.

The problem is that most of us don't take an active enough role in choosing the words we express and curating those coming into our lives. We speak without contemplating the immense force that flows from our speech. We allow the power of others' words to assail us and bring all kinds of emotional energy that affects us. This leads to blurting out something cruel in a moment of stress or constantly ingesting fearful words from the news.

Most of us are victims of the power of words. Most of us are passively participating in the labor of life without understanding the laws of language.

The solution is to be active architects in the domains of verbal expression and interpretation. We can focus on building and expanding our vocabulary as the foundation for greater self-expression, and self-love. Carefully choosing which words we express, and what emotional force we express them with.

We must also be active in our vigilance for the way others' words affect us. We can wrongly interpret the words of others based on our emotional lens. But, we can also falsely tolerate the words of others that we would be better off not exposing ourselves to and internalizing.

Don't ignore the power of words. This power will play a perpetual role in your life. Our ability to find love and joy relies entirely on the frequency of those words being sought, expressed, received, and understood.

We must not ignore the opportunity to gain a greater understanding of the words we hear and use often. Look up the definition of familiar words, and learn a greater depth and appreciation for the meanings we seldom revisit once we "know the meaning". Look up love and joy and see how that can help remind you of nuances in the words we often forget.

Some words cannot be defined by others, only by us. Success and happiness are two such words. We mustn't allow a definition of success that is not under our control our whole life. Nor must we tolerate chasing after an under-defined "happiness".

Without asking what success and happiness mean to us we are diminishing the power of those words and our ability to manifest them.

If words help shape and define our reality, then etymology is physics. Understanding the words we use regularly is as important as understanding the physical laws of nature.

1. Try to release excuses

Excuses allow you to shift blame and deny your own role in your current situation.

While you may have no control over certain events, how you respond can help influence your outcome. Taking time to examine your own responses as well as actions that may have led to the current situation may help give you actionable steps to take.

Chapter 3: Adversity

When confirmed to mental adversity, the human mind is durable. One can bend and brake components of thought and pieces of an adverse situation and create a reality that gives the individual peace of mind. For instance, an unexplainable downfall arises in one's life that slows down progress toward one's ability to process the next venture in life, meaning that this individual is not able to move past something that has happened. The individual could dwell in a state of lifelessness and become fixated on what happened and keep replaying the situation in his or her mind. Or, the individual could use the mind's ability to bend and break components of thoughts to advance through the adverse situation. A way to do this is by changing one's perspective of the situation depending on the severity of the situation or relating the situation to previous adversities and having the mindset of "what doesn't kill me will make me stronger."

Ways Successful People Push Through Adversity

Hard times happen. Getting past them is a mental game you can win.
We all face adversity from time to time, but some of us can flourish when things get difficult, while others seem to struggle to get out of bed in the morning. Successful people have found a way to jump hurdles and navigate around roadblocks that would stop others completely.
How is it that some people can bounce back and find a way to overcome misfortune and defeat? For one, they don't allow themselves to become overwhelmed with negative emotions or thoughts. They take time to process what they've been through, then they resume moving forward. Their mental fortitude lifts them to seek opportunities instead of dwelling in despair.
If you want to find a way to continue to grow and achieve a following in the hardest of times, read on. Here are 10 ways successful people push through adversity and bolster themselves, even when facing disaster.

1. Find your sense of humor.
They say laughter is the best medicine. It's your body's way of coping with stress, releasing the tension, and resetting your brain to be more positive. A good chuckle will release endorphins and dopamine, nature's feel-good chemical.
It might seem unthinkable to find anything funny when you're struggling from one of life's blows. But sometimes just stepping back and seeing the humor of the situation can help lighten your mood and allow you to move forward. You may not be chuckling amid a major setback, but give yourself some time. Finding your sense of humor when facing adversity is a healthy way to build resilience, no matter how bad your situation is.

2. Be mentally prepared.
"I am prepared for the worst, but hope for the best. Being prepared means thinking through the worst-case scenarios and considering how you would react.
What would your plan of action be if a crisis hit? Running through potential disasters regularly builds mental strength and flexibility to overcome mishaps or catastrophes in real life. It doesn't mean you should dwell on negative possibilities. But if the worst happens, having thought through how you'd react will keep you from panicking and help you stay calm and rational. It won't feel so frightening because you won't be caught completely off guard.

3. Take stock of all you've been through already.

They say what doesn't kill you makes you stronger. The hardships and misfortunes you've been through can give you confidence that you're capable of handling whatever comes your way. You've been in tough times before. How did you overcome adversity at that time? What got you through? Your past experiences can help you find your inner strength and resilience.

4. Adversity offers valuable insights.

Adversity is a great teacher. This is your chance to gain valuable insights; to truly learn from your mistakes so you'll have a better chance of success next time. However, you will have to engage in some self-reflection. Where and how did things go wrong?

Take a hard look at your planning. Did you miss something key? Consider your preparations. Were you ready for the challenges ahead? Look at your execution. Did you put in the consistent effort? Focus on areas that are within your control and ask yourself what more can you do next time.

5. Make peace with the situation.

Now is not the time to blame others for what happened. Moping around and feeling sorry for yourself will do you no good, and can sabotage your ability to come up with solutions and the next steps forward. You must consider what mistakes or missteps you might have made.

Spend time processing what you could have done differently and take responsibility for your actions. Make peace with what happened. Accept the situation for what it is, and then move on. As Steve Jobs said, "Sometimes when you innovate, you make mistakes. It's best to admit them quickly and get on with improving your other innovations."

6. Embrace adversity as a chance for opportunity.

Life is full of adversity and struggle. It's through difficult times that we learn the most important lessons in life and build resilience. Adversity often presents opportunities we might otherwise miss. Now is your chance to dig deep and face this obstacle head-on. Hard times present you with the chance to change course, reinvent yourself or find an undiscovered bridge that will get you over this hurdle.

7. Refuse to give up.

To overcome a crisis, you need to fully commit to finding a way forward. You must approach the problem determined and motivation. This will create a mindset where you look at adversity as something to be overcome and solved, not passively accepted. Sometimes dilemmas and obstacles are a chance to create alternative paths, dream bigger, push forward and take even larger leaps.

8. Have a purpose.

When life gets tough, it helps to have a crystal-clear idea of why you're doing what you're doing. If you have purpose and passion for your goals, you'll be motivated to keep pushing through until you're successful. Sometimes things happen beyond your control, and that can knock the wind out of your sails. But if you're working on something meaningful to you, you'll always find a way back to it.

9. Keep a positive mindset.

A healthy dose of optimism goes a long way when you're faced with a bad situation. It may seem cliché, but sometimes the darkest storm clouds do have silver linings. It turns out that developing a positive mindset is an important coping skill when dealing with adversity.

You indeed need to be realistic and see a situation clearly, but if you constantly negatively frame everything, you'll only see the bad. Try cultivating positivity and refuse to let pessimistic voices and naysayers invade your mind.

10. Belief in your capabilities.

People who rebound from adversity begin by believing they are capable of finding a way forward. If you feel hopeless and powerless, it's unlikely you'll find a way to be successful.

You have to have self-confidence and a strong belief in your capabilities to overcome difficult times. You have to be open-minded and willing to leverage your talent, know-how, and ingenuity to overcome adversity.

Ways to Overcome Adversity

- Release excuses New focus
- Journaling
- Block negativity
- Celebrate accomplishments
- Positive people
- Self-care
- Goal setting
- Keep trying

Benefits of adversities

Overcoming and potentially thriving from adversity isn't out of reach for anyone. It can help you become stronger and more resilient in the process.

Adversity is a hardship, problematic situation, or misfortune. It can occur to anyone, no matter who they are and what path they choose in life.

Adversity can be short-term and limited, like being denied a promotion or dealing with an acute injury or illness. Or it can be more complex and long-term, like living in poverty, having difficulty in a career path, or losing a loved one.

Getting through adversity isn't always a simple task and goes a lot deeper than slogans about getting through anything with the right mindset. The right attitude can help, but you will likely need to try different approaches to find the best solution for you.

Focusing too much on the negative can lead to a psychological phenomenon known as a self-fulfilling prophecy.

Visualization, positive self-talk, mindfulness meditation, and other strategies may help you to change your perception from a negative one to a positive one. They may also help influence a more positive future.

3. Try journaling

Journaling is the simple act of writing out what's going on along with your thoughts and your feelings. It can be therapeutic at the moment.

4. Block out the bad noise

Everyone has opinions, and not all are helpful or constructive. Some can even bring you down and make it easier to engage in self-doubt.

You can try to block out the negativity with a variety of different strategies, such as practicing self-care or setting clear boundaries, but you should use the one that works for you.

5. Celebrate your accomplishments

Whether big or small, take some time to acknowledge your accomplishments as they happen. In doing so, you can see how far you've come and help build up your self-confidence and self-esteem so you can get past whatever adversity you're currently facing.

6. Surround yourself with positive people

Positive people and those with good mindsets can help energize you. People who will praise or positively respond to your goals, ambitions, and choices can help give you the confidence to keep going.

7. Take time to take care of yourself

Sometimes you need to take some time just for yourself. While focusing on your goals and getting out of the situation can help. Taking time to engage in leisure activities can help you feel better rested and allow you to keep moving forward. You may consider engaging in activities such as:

- rest
- playing a game
- exercise
- gardening
- stretching

8. Set your own goals

Students set goals with mentors who then encouraged them to raise their goals. Research shows that the students performed worse than those who set goals without being challenged to raise them.

The researchers theorized this had two possible reasons. The first was that the goal in the raised group was too high for the student to achieve. The second theory was that the students in the raised group didn't feel ownership of their goal.

You may find that when you set your goals, they're both realistic for you and something you feel you chose. Not someone else's goal.

9. Don't be afraid to try again

Rejection, whether professional or personal, can be hard to deal with and move past. But just because one person said no or didn't like you does not mean you won't find someone who will appreciate you or your ideas.

What are the benefits of having adversities in your life?

Adversity can challenge you. While it's certainly not ideal, it can help you to learn perseverance and how to stay positive in bad situations. It can also help you learn to cope with the changes that adversity may bring.

Adversity can help you grow and learn. It can show you who you are and how you can cope with uncomfortable situations.

Types of adversity

Adversity can come in many forms. They include broad categories such as:

Emotional adversity: rejection, trouble processing emotions

Mental adversity: learning disabilities, issues with memory

Physical adversity: illness, disabilities, injury

Social adversity: trouble making friends, dealing with bullies

Financial adversity: poverty, loss of a job, trouble in career

Adversity can occur no matter where you are in life. When you face adversity, it can lead to positive changes in how you view yourself.

Strategies to deal with adversity don't work in all situations or for all people. You may find that different strategies don't work for you at all, while you can tweak others to make them your own.

A Guide to Facing Life's Challenges and Adversities

What is resilience; why is it so important, and how do you know if you're resilient enough?

Resilience is typically defined as the capacity to recover from difficult life events. Resilience is not a trampoline, where you're down one moment and up the next. It's more like climbing a mountain without a trail map. It takes time, strength, and help from people around you, and you'll likely experience setbacks along the way. But eventually, you reach the top and look back at how far you've come.

Chapter 4: What Is Resilience Theory?

People experience all kinds of adversity in life. There are personal experiences, such as illness, loss of a loved one, abuse, bullying, job loss, and financial instability. There is the shared reality of tragic events in the news, such as terrorist attacks, mass shootings, and natural disasters. People have to learn to cope with and work through very challenging life experiences.

Resilience theory refers to the ideas surrounding how people are affected by and adapt to things like adversity, change, loss, and risk.

Being resilient does not mean that people don't experience stress, emotional upheaval, and suffering. Some people equate resilience with mental toughness, but demonstrating resilience includes working through emotional pain and suffering.

Resilience isn't a fixed trait. Flexibility, adaptability, and perseverance can help people tap into their resilience by changing certain thoughts and behaviors. Research shows that students who believe that both intellectual abilities and social attributes can be developed show a lower stress response to adversity and improved performance. Resilience can be defined in terms of five principles:

- Gratitude
- Compassion
- Acceptance
- Meaning
- Forgiveness

Top Factors of Resilience

Developing resilience is both complex and personal. It involves a combination of inner strengths and outer resources, and there isn't a universal formula for becoming more resilient. All people are different: While one person might develop symptoms of depression or anxiety following a traumatic event, another person might not report any symptoms at all.

A combination of factors contributes to building resilience, and there isn't a simple to-do list to work through adversity. In one longitudinal study, protective factors for adolescents at risk for depression, such as family cohesion, positive self-appraisals, and good interpersonal relations, were associated with resilient outcomes in young adulthood.

While individual's process trauma and adversity in different ways, certain protective factors help build resilience by improving coping skills and adaptability. These factors include:

Social Support social systems that provide support in times of crisis or trauma support resilience in the individual. Social support can include immediate or extended family, community, friends, and organizations.

Realistic Planning The ability to make and carry out realistic plans helps individuals play to their strengths and focus on achievable goals.

Self-Esteem A positive sense of self and confidence in one's strengths can stave off feelings of helplessness when confronted with adversity.

Coping Skills Coping and problem-solving skills help empower a person who has to work through adversity and overcome hardship.

Communication Skills Being able to communicate clearly and effectively helps people seek support, mobilize resources, and take action.

Emotional Regulation The capacity to manage potentially overwhelming emotions (or seek assistance to work through them) helps people maintain focus when overcoming a challenge.

Research on resilience theory shows that it is imperative to manage an individual's immediate environment and promote protective factors while addressing the demands and stressors that the individual faces.

In other words, resilience isn't something people tap into only during overwhelming moments of adversity. It builds as people encounter all kinds of stressors daily, and protective factors can be nurtured.

Why Is Resilience Important?

Resilience is what gives people the emotional strength to cope with trauma, adversity, and hardship. Resilient people utilize their resources, strengths, and skills to overcome challenges and work through setbacks.

People who lack resilience are more likely to feel overwhelmed or helpless and rely on unhealthy coping strategies (such as avoidance, isolation, and self-medication). One study showed that patients who had attempted suicide had significantly lower resilience scale scores than patients who had never attempted suicide. Resilient people do experience stress, setbacks, and difficult emotions, but they tap into their strengths and seek help from support systems to overcome challenges and work through problems. Resilience empowers them to accept and adapt to a situation and move forward. Resilience is "the core strength you use to lift the load of life,"

What Are the 7 Cs of Resilience?

The 7 Cs model of resilience to help kids and teens build the skills to be happier and more resilient.

The 7 Cs model is centered around two key points:

Young people live up or down to the expectations that are set for them and need adults who love them unconditionally and hold them to high expectations.

How we model resilience for young people is far more important than what we say about it.

The American Academy of Pediatrics summarizes the 7 Cs as follows:

Competence This is the ability to know how to handle situations effectively. To build competence, individuals develop a set of skills to help them trust their judgments and make responsible choices.

Confidence Dr. Ginsburg says that true self-confidence is rooted in competence. Individuals gain confidence by demonstrating competence in real-life situations.

Connection Close ties to family, friends, and community provide a sense of security and belonging.

Character Individuals need a fundamental sense of right and wrong to make responsible choices, contribute to society, and experience self-worth.

Contribution Ginsburg says that having a sense of purpose is a powerful motivator. Contributing to one's community reinforces positive reciprocal relationships.

Coping When people learn to cope with stress effectively, they are better prepared to handle adversity and setbacks.

Control

Developing an understanding of internal control helps individuals act as problem-solvers instead of victims of circumstance. When individuals learn that they can control the outcomes of their decisions, they are more likely to view themselves as capable and confident.

The 7 Cs of resilience illustrate the interplay between personal strengths and outside resources, regardless of age.

Resilience is 'the core strength you use to lift the load of life.'

Types of Resilience: Psychological, Emotional, Physical, and Community The word resilience is often used on its own to represent overall adaptability and coping, but it can be broken down into categories or types:

- Psychological resilience
- Emotional resilience
- Physical resilience
- Community resilience

What Is Psychological Resilience?

Psychological resilience refers to the ability to mentally withstand or adapt to uncertainty, challenges, and adversity. It is sometimes referred to as "mental fortitude." People who exhibit psychological resilience develop coping strategies and capabilities that enable them to remain calm and focused during a crisis and move on without long-term negative consequences.

What Is Emotional Resilience?

There are varying degrees of how well a person copes emotionally with stress and adversity. Some people are, by nature, more or less sensitive to change. How a person responds to a situation can trigger a flood of emotions.

Emotionally resilient people understand what they're feeling and why. They tap into realistic optimism, even when dealing with a crisis, and are proactive in using both internal and external resources. As a result, they can manage stressors as well as their emotions in a healthy, positive way.

What Is Physical Resilience?

Physical resilience refers to the body's ability to adapt to challenges, maintain stamina and strength, and recover quickly and efficiently. A person can function and recover when faced with illness, accidents, or other physical demands.

Physical resilience plays an important role in healthy aging, as people encounter medical issues and physical stressors.

Healthy lifestyle choices, building connections, making time to rest and recover, deep breathing, and engaging in enjoyable activities all play a role in building physical resilience.

Resilience Training

The good news is that resilience can be learned. For example, people can build up social support networks or learn to reframe negative thoughts.

Learning to be resilient doesn't mean figuring out how to "grin and bear it" or simply "get over it." It's not about learning to avoid obstacles or resisting change.

Building resilience is a process by which people utilize flexibility to reframe thought patterns and learn to tap into a strengths-based approach to working through obstacles.

How to Build and Cultivate Resilience

It's helpful to think of resilience as a process. The following are steps that can help build resilience over time:

Develop self-awareness. Understanding how you typically respond to stress and adversity is the first step toward learning more adaptive strategies. Self-awareness also includes understanding your strengths and knowing your weaknesses.

Build self-regulation skills. Remaining focused in the face of stress and adversity is important but not easy. Stress-reduction techniques, such as guided imagery, breathing exercise, and mindfulness training, can help individuals regulate their emotions, thoughts, and behaviors.

Learn coping skills. Many coping skills can help in dealing with stressful and challenging situations. They include journaling, reframing thoughts, exercising, spending time outdoors, socializing, improving sleep hygiene, and tapping into creative outlets.

Increase optimism. More optimistic people tend to feel more in control of their outcomes. To build optimism, focus on what you *can* do when faced with a challenge, and identify positive, problem-solving steps that you can take.

Strengthen connections. Support systems can play a vital role in resilience. Bolster your existing social connections and find opportunities to build new ones.

Know your strengths. People feel more capable and confident when they can identify and draw on their talents and strengths.

How Resilient Are You?

Resilience is not a permanent state. A person may feel equipped to manage one stressor and overwhelmed by another. Remember the factors that build resilience, and try to apply them when dealing with adversity.

In general, resilient people have many of the following characteristics:

Locus of Control Focus on how you, as opposed to external forces, can control the outcome of events.

Social Support Rely on family, friends, and colleagues when needed.

Problem-Solving Skills Identify ways within your control to work and resolve a problem.
Optimism When the going gets tough, believe in your ability to handle it.
Coping Skills Find techniques to reduce stress and anxiety.
Self-Care Make your mental, emotional, and physical health top priorities.
Self-Awareness Know your strengths and weaknesses and how to put internal resources to work.

Resilience and Health Conditions

Studies have shown that characteristics of resilience, particularly social connections and a strong sense of self-worth, help people confront chronic illness.

Mental Health and Resilience

Resilience is a protective factor against psychological distress in adverse situations involving loss or trauma. It can help in the management of stress levels and depressive symptoms. Psychological resilience refers to the mental fortitude to handle challenges and adversity.

Rheumatoid Arthritis and Resilience

The research found that behavioral and emotional strategies to cultivate resilience can benefit patients with rheumatoid arthritis (RA) and other chronic diseases. One study concluded that optimism and perceived social support help improve the quality of life for RA patients.

Immunological Disorders and Resilience

Research supports the idea that physical resilience can reduce the adverse effect that stressors have on the immune system. Studies have shown that low resilience is associated with the worsening of disease, whereas high resilience is associated with better quality of life.

Digestive Conditions and Resilience

People suffering from anxiety and depression frequently report gastrointestinal distress as a primary symptom. Building resilience can reduce the stress and anxiety associated with some GI symptoms.

Skin Conditions and Resilience

Dermatologic disorders are often accompanied by anxiety and stress. Stress, in turn, can trigger flare-ups of skin-related conditions, such as psoriasis and eczema. Studies suggest that patients with conditions like psoriasis show signs of less resilience, and early intervention to build resilience can improve symptoms and management of these conditions.

Endometriosis and Resilience

Studies have linked endometriosis and chronic, potentially debilitating pain to depressive mood, anxiety, and reduced resilience. Resilience can be an important factor in reducing the effects on physical, mental, and social well-being.

Resilience in Children

Kids confront any number of challenges as they grow — from starting school and making new friends to adverse, traumatic experiences, such as bullying and abuse. "Building resilience — the ability to adapt well to adversity, trauma, tragedy, threats, or even significant sources of stress — can help our children manage stress and feelings of anxiety and uncertainty," according to the American Psychological Association (APA).

The 7 Cs model specifically addresses resilience building in kids and teens. It lists competence, confidence, connection, character, contribution, coping, and control as essential skills for young people to handle situations effectively.

Parents can help children develop resilience through positive behaviors and thoughts. The APA lists 10 tips for building resilience in young people:

- Foster social connections
- Help children by having them help others
- Maintain a daily routine
- Take breaks from sources of stress
- Teach self-care
- Set realistic goals
- Nurture a positive self-image
- Keep things in perspective
- Encourage self-discovery
- Accept change as part of life

There is no universal formula for building resilience in young people. If a child seems overwhelmed or troubled at school and home, parents might consider talking to someone who can help, such as a counselor, psychologist, or other mental health professional.

Does Gender Affect Resilience?

Studies on resilience and gender suggest that men and women may respond differently to adversity and trauma. But the results have been conflicting.

In terms of survival and longevity, women historically thrive in greater numbers than men during times of crisis such as famines and epidemics. Even when overall life expectancy rose, researchers found women outlived men between six months and four years.

On the other hand, studies have found that women are approximately twice as likely as men to develop PTSD after a traumatic event. The reason for the gender difference is unclear, but it may have something to do with a coping style for dealing with trauma.

Resilience in Women

Resilience benefits both men and women when facing challenges and adversity. However, women also draw on resilience to overcome obstacles more often placed in their ways, such as job discrimination, sexual harassment, and domestic violence.

One study found that when confronted with gender bias in the workplace, women relied on adopting male characteristics, mentoring, and intrinsic motivational factors to work through obstacles.

Resilience in Men

Resilience can protect both men and women from mental health conditions, such as depression and anxiety.

Research has found that men who lack resilience are exponentially more vulnerable to becoming severely depressed after the loss of a spouse.

Resilience in Care giving

The burden of caring for someone, such as an older adult or a chronically ill loved one, can be a tremendous source of stress and affect a caregiver's well-being.

Chapter 5: Main Idea- Challenging the mind

Challenging the human mind is an everlasting and enduring task. For instance, when we challenge the human mind, we put ourselves in a situation that requires mental endurance. This is an everlasting task because challenging the human mind allows you to go from one mentality to another based on what an individual believes is right during that stage in life. Mental endurance is more interdependent than anything. Mental endurance comes from the manifestations of the mind in order to create a standard of what's difficult and what's not. A relatively difficult task to society may not be difficult to an individual who manifests an ability to psychologically believe a "difficult task" is easy. The human mind has the ability to operate on relativity of the task to a standard. Relativity standard is based on the individual's limitations, whether these limitations are physical limitations or psychological limitations. Physical limitations are futile to accomplishing task that require work in the physical world. However, psychological limitations are self-introduced. Us as human beings have the ability to disengage psychological limitations and pursue what's desired. What's actually real is based on the individual, and we have the ability to separate negative thoughts and positive thoughts as far as mental thoughts.

Maintaining the ability to challenge the mind

Since challenging the human mind is an everlasting task, every day could be an opportunity to find a new method of getting something done more effectively. Using the mind to overcome task in a better way is an ability that is gained from maintaining the ability to challenge the mind. Consistently of the mentality allows one to evolve as an individual and keep a consistent mentality until revisions need to be made in order to survive what life puts in front of the individual. The inevitably of life is what causes the individual to scale back on his or her mentality and keeping in mind the ability to challenge the mind gives the individual the tools to manifest new ideas to solve a task. Staying alert to inevitably and instability allows one to accommodate to new circumstances and situations one is placed in as time progresses. When one loses a sense of inevitably and instability of life, he or she is doomed to withholding to principles that will not allow him or her to succeed for incoming adversities.

Maintaining core mentality when revisions are necessary

When revisions are necessary, when one's mentality resonates in his or her heart, he or she should not revise core beliefs. For instance, an individual finds him or herself surrounded by a group of new people. The group of new people has found a new way of accomplishing something more effectively by using some principles of their mentality. As an individual, you see how this group of people accomplished something more effectively than you have with the principles of their mentality. Using the same principles the group of people used, you could use this strategy to provide more efficiency toward getting what needs to be accomplished done. However, your core mentality does not need to be changed because your core mentality makes you who you are. A more specific example of this would be if one was giving a presentation for work. Since the employer prefers things to be done in a certain fashion to his or her customs, you would perform the task in a way that's favorable to the employer.

"You never know until it's too late"
   Having a steadfast set of beliefs (mentality) is easier announced than represented through actions and thought processes. With that being stated, a person could create an ideal self of what he or she chooses to believe in, but does he or she actually hold to his or her mentality? For instance, in a situation, will an individual "break his or her code" and act out of character or will he or she follow his or her beliefs? "You never know until it's too late." An individual's emotional response could cause an individual great regret.

Harnessing emotional response

When an individual takes a moment to bring his or her beliefs to mind in a situation where he or she may feel regret later, this will ensure the individual makes the best logical decision and keeps his or her integrity. "Situations are circumstantial. Mentality is enduring." "Is it worth it?"

Creating the "right" mentality to have

The "right" mentality is relative to what an individual thinks is morally just or good. When an individual adapts a mentality by applying what is the right thing to do to the best of his or her ability, he or she would not have a doubt in his or her mind that when the mentality is put to use that the best decision is being made. Furthermore, a man or woman does not know what he or she stands for then there's not an easy way for this individual to truly discover who he or she really is.

Chapter 6: Fighting negative thoughts in situations

 Fear, regret, and discouragement are all forms of humility. Humility is a natural response to something that appears foreign to an individual. Fear of the unknown is a fear that exists but doesn't have a "real" reason to exist. The unknown is the unknown for a reason and the fear associated with it can be conquered. Once an individual adopts the mentality that he or she will disregard things that are out of his or her control, this fear becomes nonexistent. The unknown does not become reality until it is made known, which is impossible to discover exactly what it is.
Regret is a form of humility that comes after the reality of a situation. Regret is brought on by having sorrow for a particular action that was committed or an event that took place. A primary way to prevent regret from stopping an individual from making progress in his or her life is to accept the consequences that came from the bad decision.

When this is done, the individual now has space in his or her mind to do the best that he or she can do to stray away from what caused them to make the decision that was made. If the individual makes the wrong decisions with the right intentions, the individual should try to find an alternate route to make ends with the right intentions by all means. Typically, there's more than one way to accomplish an objective.

Mental freedom is a venture that many have searched for since the age of philosophy started. What defines mental freedom for each individual is relative if the individual knows him or herself well enough. For instance, one reads something philosophy-oriented and gathers thoughts from what he or she just read. These thoughts become personalized if the individual has his or her own identity. Nonetheless, the author of the reading has a central message to convey in his or her reading, but the individual has applied these thoughts to his or her circumstances in life. In this process, the reader has gained the central message of the philosophy-oriented reading and deeper processing of the message the author conveys in the reading has a central message to convey in his or her reading, but the individual has applied these thoughts to circumstances in life. In this process, the reader has gained the central message of the philosophy-oriented reading and deeper processing of the message the author conveys in the reading has been made.

Ways to Stop Spiraling Negative Thoughts from Taking Control

One gradual habit can become a powerful mental tool

With most external wounds, treatment is usually pretty straightforward. For instance, when you cut your finger, you can use antibacterial cream and a bandage, and after some time, the wound will close. You're pretty much good to go.

Treating your thought processes isn't as easy or prescriptive. Especially if they stem from general anxiety, depression, or another mental health condition.

Negative thought patterns are like a paper cut you keep getting when you have only a vague idea of what's causing it. Or maybe you don't notice the cut at all... until it starts to sting.

Each person, depending on their condition and triggers, will require different approaches to medication, psychotherapy, and lifestyle changes. And when therapy is out of reach, it can be difficult to get fast treatment.

One gradual habit that might help is making mental shifts

Shifting the way you think means you're consciously stopping an established thought pattern. You re-evaluate how you reflect on a situation, or even what you think about, to focus on something else.

It's like switching gears in your brain so your train of thought isn't just looping and relooping.

In a lot of ways, this is about undoing a lot of negative behaviors and mental programming you may have learned from others. For example, if you grew up thinking you had to be the best in school and life, you're likely programmed for stressful perfectionism.

What situation is causing your anxiety?

Creating a thought record is essentially putting your thoughts to the test. Start by asking yourself who, what, where, and when. This'll help you describe what happened while sticking to the facts instead of your feelings.

- Who were you with?
- What were you doing?
- Where were you?
- When was it?

2. What's your mood in this situation?

Describe your moods in one word and then rate the intensity of these moods on a percentage scale that equals 100. For instance, if you're handing in a work project, your moods may include:

- irritated
- nervous
- guilt, perhaps if it's being handed in late

In this case, if nervousness — which falls into anxiety — is your predominant mood, you'd rate it around 80 percent. Irritation and guilt would then fill up the remaining 20 percent.

The percentage doesn't have to be perfect — just go with your gut. The main point of rating them is to see how much of your thoughts were influenced by a specific type of mood — an anxious mood versus a guilty one, for example.

3. What are the automatic thoughts running through your mind?

This is the most important step in your thought record: List the thoughts and images that popped into your mind relating to that situation. Try to remember what you were thinking at the time.

Automatic thoughts can include:

- *I'm so dumb.*
- *I'm going to mess this up.*
- *Nobody likes me.*
- *The world is an awful place.*
- *I can't cope with this.*
- *I'm going to end up alone.*

If you find yourself caught with ANTs like these, breaking down the situation into "tasks" may help shift your mindset away from the predominant mood controlling your thoughts.

For example, evaluate why the situation is causing you to think "I'm going to mess this up" before you begin.

If it's a work situation, ask whether you're afraid because of past projects that have gone awry? How is this situation different from past projects?

Play out the worst-case scenario and see how you feel about it. Break down your emotions and moods to see if your anxiety or automatic thoughts have any legs to stand on.

As you dig into the details, you might discover that this work situation is independent of your past and future.

Identifying your automatic thoughts is the first step in gaining control of your emotions. What are you telling yourself? Now how can you change it?

How can you change your negative thinking?

Once you discovered your automatic thoughts, it's time to put them on trial.

Is there evidence to support this thought? If this evidence is based on the past, why does this apply to this new experience?

You want to focus on credible evidence — not feelings or thoughts. Then it's time to focus on evidence that doesn't support your thought.

Let's run through one to show you how it works.

Thought: I'm going to mess this up.

Credible evidence for my thought:

- I made a mistake early on that set this project back by a few weeks.

- I don't have strong skills as a presenter.

- I've never done this big of a project on my own before.

Credible evidence against my thought:

- My manager and I discussed the timeline of the project and came to an understanding.

- I've been practicing my presentation for over two weeks and have practiced in front of a co-worker who gave me helpful feedback.

- I know the topic, so I should be able to answer any questions that come up.

Now it's time to find an alternative to your original thought

You have your evidence for both sides, so now it's time to be a judge. A helpful tip is to act as if you're judging the thought of a friend rather than your own thought.

Now, you can find an alternative, more balanced thought. This new thought will consider all of the evidence for and against you and give your wiser mind a shot at running the show.

For instance:

- "I have made mistakes, but in general I work very hard."

- "I'm genuinely trying my best."

- "I've gotten good feedback so far and my manager trusts me to do this."

Reminder: Everything can be broken down into smaller, more manageable tasks. Find a place where you can pause and check-in with your thoughts to see where in the process you may be able to give yourself a break.

Acknowledge the emotional roller coaster or burden when you experience it

Like recognizing ANTs, there's also power in simply acknowledging that you feel overwhelmed. Don't automatically put yourself in defensive mode and whirl into an anxiety tailspin. Whether it's from stress, anxiety, or another condition, the first step to combating mental strain is welcoming it.

I know what you're thinking: Why would I ever welcome all the shakes and jitters that take over my brain and body?

Because embracing it can take a lot less energy than dreading it.

Instead of using extra energy to forcibly fight back, realize that this reaction means you're encountering something that's important to you. It also means you may not have to force yourself to operate at 100 percent all the time. That's exhausting.

Understanding your anxiety and what it means is one of the first steps to managing the stress that comes with it. You may discover that there's a trigger. When you find it, you can act to avoid or you may find yourself spending less time dreading it.

Spend more time asking yourself, "Oh, hello anxiety, what do we need to do to function together today?" and you might end up fighting against yourself less through the stressful event.

Reminder: There's always another option — even if it means opting out or saying no. If your anxiety or stress is based on a situation, ask yourself if you can opt out. Chances are you can!

Challenge yourself to make small steps instead of forcing positive thoughts
Making mental shifts isn't about turning "I feel sad" into "I feel happy."

First off, if this worked, general anxiety would be far easier to treat and could be thought out of existence.

There will be times when, no matter how hard you try to change your thought pattern, you can't. And during those times, it's important to remember that simply recognizing the thought, or acknowledging it — as mentioned above — is enough.

It's OK to feel sad. It's OK to feel anxious. Take a break and give yourself another day.

When you do have the energy, you can slowly work toward moving past initial thoughts of "I feel sad" to recognizing there may be a problem and considering a workaround.

The more you remind yourself of these things, the more your thoughts will untangle so you can reach the next stage of growth and strength.